Oneness of Soul

by Casey S. Leasure

Copyright © 2011 Casey S. Leasure
First Edition 2012
Revised Version Printed 2013
ISBN: 978-0-615-57663-3
Printed in the United States of America
Library of Congress TX 7-623-450

The illustration on the cover of this book
is out of the public domain and through the
courtesy of the Library of Congress
Pygmalion and Galatea painting by Gerome 1890

THIS BOOK IS PUBLISHED
BY
CASEY S. LEASURE

Dedication

Every living creature has a soul.
In each one of those souls is a unique work of art
designed by the Consciousness of Oneness.
Each soul has a journey, a dance, a song, and a
story. Every soul is on the path, moving to the
sacred dance of the song they hear, writing its
chapter in the story of the journey to the
Great Compassion in Life.
~ Casey ~

Contents

Pages

1

Merging Souls of Love

In my dream I carved my beloved from a stone of marble.
With each strike of my mallet as pieces of stone fell I saw a past life where we had loved.
As I carved I could hear her laughter and song coming from the stone.
To the image I danced the sculptor's sacred dance and chanted the dreamer's prayer of love.
In love with an idea carved from my desires, I watched as angels came to awaken the soul of my statue.
I kissed her and felt the soft moist lips of my dream come to life.
And we danced the sacred dance of an eternal love.
When I awoke, I was but a small stone in the palm of a woman's hand, as her thoughts reflected on an eternal love of a man that loved her so passionately.

*Let a man call upon the angel of love to guide his
lips as they dance upon the texture of her skin.
Let his hands gently climb the desires of her body as
his fingers play a melody on her, as though she
were a harp sent to him from heaven.
Let a woman dress his soul with her heart as she
moves with man like the willow tree in a gentle
breeze.
Let a woman anoint a man's body with the oils of
her love, and the song they create will be heard by
the Gods of the Universe.
These Lovers of a lost treasure.*

*I cut through the veil of my dreams one night
to see just what orchestrated my visions as I slept.
And there before me was a painted woman,
floating gently in the abyss of my thoughts.
Her beauty was intoxicating, as I watched the
paintings move and change designs on her body,
as if one dream led into another.
No words were spoken, no sound was heard, but a
flow of magical movement between her body and
soul I watched.
Was this my dream maker?
Was this what guided me between the worlds of
conscious and unconscious breaths?
Slowly she danced as her eyes called my soul, yet my
body could not touch her, only my breath,
only my eyes.
So passionately I loved the Muse behind the veil
of my dreams.
Like a potter who sits at his wheel and creates a
vase, or an artist who stands before his canvas and
paints a master piece, the dream maker molds and
paints my dreams.
So I say to you, now when I dream, I step behind
the veil to commune with that which turns the wheel
and paints the canvas.
For I have seen what calls me between the worlds of
my conscious and unconscious breath.*

I don't just love you when it rains.
I love you when the lighting strikes
and the thunder roars.
As that is what I feel when I kiss you.
When I kiss you,
It is as if, inside my body
I splash like a thousand rain drops.
Harmoniously hitting a tin roof.
Grabbing each other and holding on
with their last breath, as if they will never
kiss again.
Yes, when I kiss you I am rain.

*There are no words that can properly
dress my love for you.
So I stand with no voice, my love
is naked before you.
My whispers but a breath, my eyes are but
the hands I caress you with.
It will be my soul that weaves through your
heart and through your body.
As it is your scent I taste when I think
of you my love.*

You cannot catch the wind my love
nor can you stop the rain.
But if you will close your eyes my love
you will feel my soul in the air and
a thousand of my kisses will fall
upon your body.

*What secrets does the moon whisper as I walk the
desert in her light?
And who will interpret the coyotes riddle calling me
from behind the rock?
What circles above me as I wander across the dry
desert air, is it demons or angels, is it a song without
a melody?
I look to the stars and raise my hand to the sky and
think; if I could run my fingers across the stars of
the galaxy it would read like a record of our
universe written in braille.
The moon whispers and the coyote howls and yet it
is all nothing more then the echo of my own voice I
hear calling to the night.
Calling me to dance.
It is here, I feel like a mad man, safe and
understood.
It is here, I wait for her return promised to me so
many life time's ago.
My thoughts are the desert's thoughts and my
breath cries not for what I think.
The moon will comfort me and the coyote will keep
me company as I wait for her return,
another thousand years.*

*When the sun rays stretch through the sky and lay
upon the earth I feel your love for me.
Yes my darling let my hands be like a river,
smoothly flowing over the curves and depths
of your body.
Let me kiss you like the hummingbird that drinks
from the beautiful honeysuckle flower and tastes the
sweet essence of life.
For it is when I hold you and we kiss I understand
why the stars fill the sky at night, and why the
clouds dance when the wind blows.
Let us breathe as one, I will be the music and you
will be the words as we write our song of love
for one another.*

10

*No my beloved, I will not write a message in a bottle
and cast it to the sea in hopes that someday it will
find its way to you.
I shall kneel before the river and write my love for
you upon the flowing waters.
And as it flows across the country, the farmers will
irrigate their crops with my love for you.
And the wild animals of the country side shall drink
it from the river and the fishermen shall catch it to
feed their families with my love for you.
And by the time it reaches the sea, all that lives and
grows throughout the land will have tasted how
great my love for you is.
It will be then my beloved that all will sing about my
love and it will be then, that my love will find you.*

I remember her asking me, how do you even know
we're supposed to be together?
And I looked at her and said,
Because my love, when I look into your eyes
I see my soul.

There are no words to my prayers
There is no sound to my music
And yet my love, in my heart
You are the song I pray, the melody I hear
I stand a naked spirit on the edge of silence
My thoughts cascading down your body
Soft is your breath I feel as I close my eyes
Gentle are the whispers I kiss you with
As I hold you with my love, and say, no words
But play a silent song to the night's air
As I lay with you in my memories.
Yes my love these are the echoes
of my love for you.

There once was a monster, an ugly beast in the night's air who screamed violently at the shadows on the moon.
And all lovers who could hear would shutter in fear and lose sight of their passion for each other.
One night a young maiden heard his screams as she sat at her window enjoying the cool breeze that touched her face.
But what she heard was fear and sadness calling to a lost love.
So to the night's air she sang a beautiful song of lover's holding each other in a silent love, being in the arms of each other and no longer separated from their passion and love.
The monster, now frozen in the song, touching his lips and chin with his fingers as he looked up at the moon with a tear and sighed deeply.
As it was a thousand years ago they took his love from him, and now he heard her singing the song, of her return to him.

What spirits will the shadows ride across
The fields of the lover's dream?
Who will hear the music in the garden,
In the songs that play as they kiss?

Like echoes of ecstasy cascading down
From the stars upon a passionate love,
Two who hold each other in rhythm
Of their breath.

Be it night, or light of day, the eyes of
These lovers are blind to all things.
But that which calls their passion to merge,
And their flesh to blend as one.

Their blending thoughts are like a ship
That sails upon the sea, they will sway
In the arms of each other.
Clinging to the soul of eternity.

As their love will be the conception of a
Thousand lives with a thousand masks.
And yet their soul will always remember
Their first kiss.

Love followed me,
Every corner I turned there it was.
Waiting for me, laughing and dancing
So I surrendered, and love took me.

*I looked into a rose and I saw the image of your
body lying there and as the fragrance of the rose
filled the air.
It was as if I could taste the sweetness of your kiss
once again.*

Yes my love,
I hear the music of the falling rain.
Let us dance under the rain drops as they fall.
Let me kiss you, as I hold you in my arms.
Wet is the autumn air, wet are my lips as I taste
your love for me.
Like the rain that falls from the sky
let my love fall upon your body.
And I will be the ecstasy of your desire,
And you my love,
will be the answer to my prayers.

*I raised my hand to the sky and touched the face of
all life!
It was then I knew all things were connected and I
was one with you.
I vowed my love to you for eternity, and the universe
heard my words.
The sky grabbed my hand and I rode the wind to
your heart.
And it was there we merged into a song of laughter
and joy as we whirled through the sky like eagles in
a courtship of love.
Raise your hand my love, life awaits us.*

If I were just a breath, you my love would be my air.

When a man loves a woman, with all his heart,
he is like a river.
And she is like the soft whispers that call him home.
But when a man loves a woman with his soul,
he becomes like the sea and she becomes
the voice that raises the tides of his love.

Open the door to the calling of your heart,
step across the threshold into your secret desires.
Let the untamed colors of your soul dance
in the arms of a wild fire you call love.

*The ocean is my soul and the sand is my body.
You my love are my oxygen, my next breath.*

*Pull the anchor from the wreckage of
your past my friend.
Raise your sails and set your course
for the shining star.
Journey the sea of your Soul,
upon your ship of love.
And let the winds carry you to the
land of passion and love.*

*Let us honor the oneness of our love.
We will dance beneath the sun, as we kiss the sky
and wrap ourselves in a blanket of joy.
As our hearts ride the wind the rhythm of our
song sways in the trees.
And our love will shelter us from the storm.*

Let me hold you,
Like a prayer in my heart.
And I will love you,
Like a beautiful song and melody.
Be still my love,
And let me feel your soft breath
Upon my skin.
You are like the song that awakens my heart,
When I hold you.

*When Spirits merge and we connect, it is like
floating in the joy of love.
In the quietness of his life he is at peace seeking
nothing more than to be still.
Listen to source of all life move through you
Showing you the one consciousness of love.*

I once heard a flower ask a butterfly
What do you think created us.
And the butterfly answered it was are love
For one another that created us.

*I just received notice that I've been diagnosed with
a rare eye disease called Angelic Blindness
It means I can only see you through the eyes of
love.
This virus is often found in children but is most
often out-grown as they get older.
Let us pray I do not out-grow mine!*

Does a flower dream of being loved,
Passionately held and caressed?
And when a gardener prunes the roses
And smells their fragrance, will he dream of
The woman he loves and hold her
Iin the garden of his heart?
Awaken to the Kingdom of Love my flower,
Your gardener awaits you.

Do not stop my love from dreaming in this world
or the next.
Like my garden, my love dreams wild and free.
So lay with me as my dreams drip sweet thoughts of
love and ecstasy on to our mortal bodies as we sleep
on a journey through my garden.

Ashes to ashes
Dust to dust
My body they will bury.
But my love for you
Echoes throughout time,
In the birth of every flower.

*For a thousand years I stood on the shore gazing
up at the stars as they kissed the night with
their passion.*

*Dreaming as the waves of the sea caressed the
beach's sand, touching me feet, pulling me into
their dance for one another.*

How I longed for this union between two souls.

*For a thousand years I stood upon the shores in the
morning dawn and watch the sun kiss the sky in a
sacred dance that would last the whole day.*

*And so it was I stood on the shore before the Gods
and sacrificed my flesh to the sea.*

*To the stars and to the sky as I prayed to the Gods
that I too would have this love of self and another
soul.*

*The sky shook, and the sea roared as the Gods
laughed and I melted into the dream of my union
between two souls.*

*For the next one thousand years as the waves
caressed the beach, I awoke to your love for me
as we kissed in the union between our souls.*

*And yet our journey will carry us endlessly through
the light of our Heavenly Consciousness.
Where our dreams and our thoughts cascade down
upon us.
To meditate is to listen to the silent voice from above
the stars, and to dream is to dance with that
which calls to us from the Light.
My flesh and bone is my cocoon, my soul is the
brilliant colors of light that will emerge into the
garden we call eternity.*

A bridge worthy of crossing demands a sound and solid structure at both ends.
The wise understand this to be true in their relationships.
As it also will be destined to crumble in time with use, if both sides are not equally sound and secured within themselves.

When music is created
Does God give it a soul
And when these souls merge
Do not the Angels
Dance upon the stars
When a man lies with
A woman and their bodies touch
It is then music
Is created and the Angels
Dance with delight

*We should never feel separate from the
Kingdom of Love.
Let nothing influence you that can change
what your heart knows.
The journey through eternity is one of light
and love, nothing else can or does exist past
soul and heaven are one.*

What does the wind feel when she dances with the sky?
What does the sky feel when he holds the rain?
If I kiss you, will you turn to rain?
Your love for me is like the wind my darling,
when I hold you like the sky.

Open the door to the calling of your heart,
Step across the threshold into your secret desires.
Let the untamed colors of your soul dance
In the arms of a wild fire you call love.

Attraction is as much about two Souls
As it is about a timeless dance.

I remembered her asking me, when you go into your
next life what do you want to remember
from this one?
And I said,
My love, I want to remember how warm and gentle
your kisses were on a cold winter's morning.

As lovers view the stars with their naked eyes,
they will know there is a kingdom of heaven.
And the Poet will soar throughout the galaxies,
as he writes the Song of God.

*Last night as I watched the sun set it reminded me
of the time she asked me,
How long do you think our love will last?
And I said,
As long as there is breath in God,
I will be in love with you my darling.*

My love, if you were only a memory in my heart,
I would walk my path alone.
And I would wrap myself in that memory and when
the world looked back at me they would say
"This man is whole and complete, for he wears a
true love."

How many life times did she tell me?
Kiss my lips for they are poisoned.
Listen to my whisper as they steal your last thought.
Lay upon my body as I will make you my offering to
the Gods.

I have watched her dance upon the desert sand
beneath the moon lit night.
I have seen her stand upon the great seas as the
storm's whirled my boat.
Her breath I have felt on my face as I walked the
mystic forest.
From the fire I build, I hear her song calling me to
come, come to her heart.
Wet from the rain, I have looked to the rainbow and
seen her sit upon it, laughing with hand extended
calling me to join her.
Was it not in the snow I walked lost, confused and
scared yet through the blizzard I see her, with the
snow owl perched upon her arm as our eyes met?
Her warm voice speaking to me eases my pain.
Yet I am carried by two Angels and assured it is not
a dream, but an awakened state of love
Yes! I see now, in the meadow not far away,
surrounded in light, dancing and singing she awaits
my return home.

Last night I woke up and saw a shadow
Dancing in the night outside my window.
I thought it was you. It made me so happy
That I went back to sleep and we danced
In my dreams till morning.

To cross a bridge anticipating your lover awaits you on the other side, is the journey of the poem.

He knows the consciousness of their soul,
The breath of all life, his heart and mind are free.
In the free fall of life, he lays back unafraid.
Her presences floating upon him,
Embraces his truth.

As I looked at the frost on the window this morning, I remembered her asking me when you go into your next life what do you want to remember from this one?
And I said, my love, I want to remember how warm and gentle your kisses were on a cold winter's morning.

I watched a flower stand naked before the Sun
Slowly it swayed back and forth in the breeze
I closed my eyes to get a closure look and saw her
standing beneath the clouds, her hair gently moving
in the wind.
Deeply I felt the beat of the drums as the echoes
chanted in my mind,
As the Sun slowly pulled her closer to the Stars and
the echoes called.
I ran across the field arms stretched out ... reaching
to the sky,
The wind pushed me to the edge of the cliff I felt no
fear, only love
I jumped,
One word ... her name I called
I grabbed a sun ray and clung to it with all my
might
As if, in an abyss of light I saw her hand reach out
for me, I let go of the sun ray, and to the fall I came,
I felt no fear only love
One word ... my name, I heard her call
Falling, falling, falling I felt,
There were no echoes left to hear,
no sun rays left to grab.
I opened my eyes,
naked I stood before the sun, swaying back and
forth with the breeze,
A flower in my hand, I wait for her........

Last night as I looked up at the stars and I heard a distant whisper.
As I looked closer and saw a shooting star across the night's sky …..
And I remembered, before she left that last time she said, "the next time you see me I shall be dancing across the sky for you."

*She giggled, silly man, the music stopped playing
and your still dancing.
I said my love, when I'm holding you the music
never stops.*

Yes my love,
I can say that I love you.
But what do you feel when
I just silently look into your eyes?
Because that is what I am really saying.

Wash away the prejudice, the differences, the lies,
Bathe in the Spirit of truth.
Cleanse yourself of all that separates you from life.
We are all creatures of one source,
Crossing each other's path, touching hearts.

I remember one evening
we were watching the sun set.
And she asked me,
How well do you feel you know me?
And I said,
My darling, for so many life times I have known you
as my beloved and I have known you as well as the
butterfly knows the flower holds the sweet nectar
they seek to sustain life.

To stand on the edge of love and jump is to trust the wind with your heart.
Love is not a map or a single path, but is like the sky and opens to all who take the risk for the joy of flight.

She once asking me,
Do you listen to me when I'm talking?
And I said,
My darling listening to you feeds my
hungry heart and quenches my thirst
for your company.

If a woman asks you,
How much is my kiss worth?
Tell her,
My love, if the stars in the galaxy were used as
currency, there would not be enough of them to pay
for even one kiss from you.

One night before we went to sleep
She asked me,
What do you dream about when you sleep?
And I said my darling,
I always dream about holding you as we
dance in the kingdom of my heart.

Was it the life before this one?
Or was it the life before all lives
That they loved so trustingly.
No form can separate this love.

*We were walking down the sidewalk one evening
and past an old theater.
As we stopped to see what was showing she asked
me….
What would you say was the greatest movie you ever
saw?
And I turned to her and said,
The one that plays in my mind when I think of you
my love.*

When I think of my love for you,
My shadow dances upon the clouds and the
mountains grow like flowers towards the sun.
When I think of my love for you,
My spirit soars with the eagles as if it were a song in
the wind and the air is filled with an angel's breath
of honey.
When I think of my love for you,
The rain falls from the heavens like liquid songs
poured upon the ground.
And my passion runs like a wild beast on a full
moon night, engulfed by the scent of your body and
my desire to take you.

This morning I went to the Farmer's Market,
I could smell the fresh herbs in the air.
I felt a light breeze and a tug on my heart and
I heard her voice whisper to me,
Do you think my garden is magical?
And I said to the whisper, yes my darling
I think everything you do is magical.

To kiss her is but a silent poem of my lips.
To hold her is to wear art upon my body.
To look into her eyes is the journey of my soul.
To make love, to her is to call upon the
Kingdom of Heaven.

And when we meet my darling,
Let my lips touch the sweetness of your heart.
As I will use my hands to caress you as though I
were an artist sculpting a Goddess from clay.
And I will hold you as though I were a wolf on the
edge of the forest holding the majestic light of the
morning dawn.
And when we meet my darling, let our spirits merge
as our Souls breathe as one.
For I will bring unto you the true gift created by the
Gods that only a woman like you could taste.

I remember holding her and she asked me,
What does it feel like when you hold me?
And I said, my love ...
When I hold you it is as if I have wrapped myself in
a warm blanket of life weaved by the angels of
heaven and anointed in holy oil by the
Divine Goddess of Love.

Once upon a sky
A man soared in love
In a dream above the clouds
In the heart, of the sun he gazed.

Caressing his thoughts of her
He would glide through the air
An open heart thirsting for her love
Above the silence, he will make love to her.

Like an angel of his desire,
The fruit upon his palate she will lay
An open heart of love, a breath in the sun
His lips will whisper soft kisses upon her flesh.

For he has not forgotten how the rain
Kisses the petals of a flower
Or how the sun dances upon the pond
Just as he remembers the melody of the night
He remembers the sweet nectar of her love for him.

Today I looked into a rose and I saw the image of your body lying there and as the fragrance of the rose filled the air.
It was as if I could taste the sweetness of your kiss once again.

If I were an Angel, I would descend from
The Kingdom of Heaven.
To you I would embrace and awaken the
Desires of your dreams.
And as you slept I would enter the forest of your
Journey and lift you upon my wings to carry you
Across the shadows to the brightest star in the
Universe I would bring you.
It is there I would dip you in the ecstasy
Of my love for you.

When I was walking through the park I thought I heard you laughing from behind a tree.
When I went to go look, there was only butterflies playing in the air.

As I reach midway on my bridge, I lean into the wind my love.
I hear your whispers calling me and my pace is steadily forward as I see the beauty of your essence awaiting me in the meadow of our dreams.

*Like a boat upon the water I sail
In your love when I hold you.
And when I lay my kisses upon your body
It feels as if the wind has pushed my sails
And carried me down a river of love.
So let me be the boat and you can be the river
And we will be one in our movement of love.*

There once was a beast that ran wild in the forest night. Who screamed and howled in a fearless anger at the emptiness and loneliness of his forest. And yet when he slumbered, it was in his dreams that a Muse would come and sing a lullaby of an enchanted love that danced in the field of romance and passion that eased his pain and desires.

Who is this woman dancing in the wind?
That moves so gently across the sand.
What is she singing, that melody from long ago?
Why can I not touch her, this mirage I thirst for?
What prayer can I say to bring her to me with no
words to speak?
Where has the wind gone, was this just a dream?
Do not wake me as I must kiss her lips for my heart
to keep breathing.

When a man loves a beautiful flower he will instinctively not want to change even one petal on it. Let him love his woman the same way.

Today I stood in the Farmers Market looking at all the delicious fruits, and I felt a soft gentle breeze.
And I remembered the time she asked me,
If I were your favorite fruit which one would I be?
And I said,
My love, you would be like a ripened mango with your texture so lovely to touch and as I tasted your fruit your juices would spill over my palate and quench my thirst for your love.
As if it were a dish served only to the Gods.

I was looking at my reflection in the pond, and it reminded me of the time she and I went swimming, and as I pulled her up next to me, I whispered "My love let me baptize you in my love, let me taste your sweet love for me, and I will merge upon you like the water around us, and we will fill our cup with passion and quench our thirst for each other."

When a mirror sleeps, what are its dream, where does it go?
Who speaks to the mirror and calls it to dance in between the worlds?
Do the stars vainly stand before the mirror, and what about angels, can they see themselves in all their glory and beauty?
Ah yes, so it is …..
The mirror dreams of holding the reflection of the Soul for all thoughts.
As it follows you in your dreams.

With compassion for all life he guards over her.
Gazing into her eyes at the reflection of past lives.
He remembers how many times they have journeyed
this path together.
Souls intertwined for eternity he thinks.
So precious each time, so unique in the roles they
live.

*As I walked in the park I watched a butterfly
sipping nectar from a flower, soon another one
came and joined her.
It reminded me of the time she said,
In my next life, I want to come back as a butterfly,
and spend my days sipping nectar from flowers.
I smiled and said,
Yes my love of course, and I shall join you.*

It is not the air I breathe when I am with you,
but love that I inhale.
For I am the Jaguar and you are my forest,
the sanctuary of my passion, my lust.
Your scent flows into my veins like sunrays
pulsating down into the earth.
Your soft words are like that which calls the
lotus to rise from beneath the waters and
kiss the sky.
When I lay with you my love, it is like the
sunset on the horizon that pulls lovers into the
night, and wraps them in a blanket of stars
on a warm summer's night.

Who is that you hear running in the forest that moves not one single leaf?
Who is that whispering your name but makes no sound to follow?
And who makes your body rock back and forth to the rhythm of a song that falls with the rain?
Whose warm breath do you feel on your skin as your body feels the lustrous rush?
It is I my love, as I have returned from your dream.

*This morning I watched two doves sitting side by
side on a branch outside my window.
And it reminded me of a time when I sat on a park
bench with my love and she asked me,
So what exactly are we, this you and I thing we
have, are we soul mates, or are we twin souls?
And I looked at her and said,
No my love, we are just ….. Soul.*

If I were a river,
I would flow into your heart
And fill you with the joy of my love.
If I were a river,
I would carry you upon my waters
Like the sky carries the clouds
And I would hold you like a beautiful song
In every thought I had.
If I were a river,
You would be the sea
Of which I journeyed so long to be with.
And when we touched we would blend
As if we were echoes of the heart
Calling to one another in a dream
Of a passionate love.
If I were a river.

She is everywhere,
Her beauty, her silence,
Sometimes I can feel her
Breath touch my face
As I walk down the street.
Yet, she eludes me each
Time I think, I can get close to her.

My Muse,
She is an Angel,
Who compels me to write her story,
So it is,
My Love
Let my lips sing of you,
As I lay myself upon the altar of
Your heavenly body.

The Path of Light

Once upon a time,
When there was no time or space.
In a land,
Where there was no soil or physical matter.
All creatures of light joyed in delight with their
Awakened State of being.

89

I watched a hungry sparrow pecking at the snow as it hopped upon the white sheet that covered the ground.

When it flew away the prints on the snow looked as if it were an ancient prayer.

But I could not read it for I am ignorant to the scriptures of bird and God.

So I asked the Sun …. Sun can you read this?

Do you know the words to this ancient prayer?

The Sun said yes I can, and peered down upon the prints in the snow.

I waited patiently to hear the answer, but all I saw were the words melt into the ground.

In anger I shouted, Sun! What did it say?

But the Sun left and the Moon came.

For many days and nights I wondered what that prayer had said.

One day I awoke and winter had ended and spring was now upon me.

And where there was once a strange language written in the snow, I now saw a small bush with wild berries growing.

A small flock of sparrows were feasting on them.

And I saw I was no longer ignorant to the ancient prayers between bird and God.

*Once while walking beside a river, love heard a cry
coming from behind a tree.*
*When love went to go look, he saw anger on the
ground crying.*
Love asked anger why are you crying?
*And anger answered I have never seen anything
beautiful; I have never seen lovers kiss, or a baby
sleeping in its mothers arms.*
*I have never even seen the union between the sun
and a flower.*
*Love thought for a minute, and then plucked his
eyes out and placed them in the face of anger.*
*Anger rejoiced in his new vision, now able to see
beauty.*
*Then he turned to love and said a thousand blessing
I pray for you my dear friend.*
But now what will you do?
As now you cannot see that which is so beautiful.
*And love replied, my beautiful friend I no longer
use my eyes to see beauty, but use only my heart, as
it is my heart that truly sees the beauty in all things.*

Who is the voice in the meadow?
Said the blue butterfly to the soul
But the voice that whispered to you in your cocoon.
Said the soul.
What is the hunger I feel so deeply that calls me to
journey?
Said the blue butterfly
It is the fragrance of the flowers that rise in the air
and the sweet nectar of their blossoms that call you.
Said the soul.
Like a melody in your memory, a song that colored
your wings, is the voice of your journey.
Tailored is your desire to love, and the experience of
love is mapped in the meadow you follow.
As the rain cannot wash it away nor will the sun dry
it up to be lost in the wind, is this path of love that
waits for you.
Said the soul
And so it is, as the song of the rising sun greets the
awakened and the warm wind blows across the land,
the blue butterfly dances her sacred dance across
the sky with soul.
As she listens to the voice on a path of eternal love.

*I stood on a street corner on a sunlit day, waiting
for the clouds to pass and the wind to stop.*
*And it was there I saw an old woman dancing in the
street with not a sound around her.*
*Her hands mystically weaving a garment to the
rhythm of her thoughts, as her legs moved so gently
like flowers swaying with the wind.*
*With her eyes slightly closed she looked to the sun,
head tilted and smiling, she danced in the street.*
*It was I that felt awkward and out of place and not
properly dressed for the occasion I watched.*
*I shouted old woman! From where does this music
come?*
*Hush ... she whispered, as she flowed up and down
in the middle of the street.*
*I'm reading she said, leaping over unseen objects,
bowing to unseen spirits, spinning in a circle she
moved so lightly.*
*On the sidewalk I stood where the rain had not
fallen, and I shouted old woman you hold no book,
no pages with ink!*
*But I will buy you a bowl of hot soup and then you
will not feel so lost and insane.*
*shhhhh! She said, I am reading and the words feed
my hunger.*
*Her hands motioned as if she were a conductor
leading a great symphony and her feet moved as if
she were a ballerina.*
*Laugh I could not, scared I was, thinking what
ghosts would haunt this poor old woman and
command her thoughts like a puppet on a string?*

*Aw yes old woman I shouted, now I see the book
and the pages you read with a half-smile I paid
my face to muster up to wear.*
*The old woman stopped and opened her eyes to look
at me and said I hold no book, there is no ink and
you see not what I read.*
*To her dance she returned in a different world on
the street she moved.*
*To her I shouted then what book is it you dance to
old woman?*
*What words do you hear like a song that causes you
to dance in the street like a foolish old drunk?*
*Her laughter echoed in my ears like a bell ringing
in the sky as she replied, it is the book of God I'm
reading, as you watch me here and now.*
*The sacred text written only upon the heart and
spoken only by the soul.*
*As if it were a choir of Angels, we will hear the true
written words that no book of man holds with ink!*
*As many a cloud had passed and the wind had
stopped blowing long ago, it was the street I could
not cross and the corner I could not leave.*
*As I watched the old woman read her book, there
were no more words to shout.*
*My eyes followed the rhythm of her movement, my
ears no longer deafened to the melody of the book
she read.*
*On my heart the written words I saw as my soul
spoke like a choir of angels to me.*
*To my knees I fell, my hands cupped to my face to
catch my cries.*

*For long ago as a child I remembered, how I read
this book she reads.*
Lifted by a hand of love so gentle was her touch.
*As I rose from my knees the old woman held me and
in the street we danced the Book of God.*
*Brave I am not, but free from the lies of men I now
see, as I dance in the streets the words I read*
*For I know; the heart is the only book God ever
signed.*

Each night as we sleep we are visited by angels who carry us to a land of love in a sea of light.
They lay us upon a breathing heart and bathe us in the oneness of all life.
It is there we see our journey home and know every soul is an eternal part of this heart, intertwined into eternity.
I know this, because I awoke when the angel came for me.

Hallowed is the ground the healer walks upon.
For each step is taken in the Light along the path.
Like the Magus who follows the stars.
The healer will follow the whisper of the Light.

*For only the starfish to greet the seahorse in an
ocean of oneness and to know there is no
separation, but an illusion of differences is to
understand the love of creation.*

*Who will hear the voice of the forest once all the
trees are gone?
Who will dance beneath the moon when all the stars
have disappeared?
What language will speak the word of God when the
world goes deaf?
It shall be the Poet's heart who writes the whispers
in the light, for the heart hears all things, and never
stops dancing.*

I am created through love and truth.
But not so, am I raised by my village.
In time, I will know this.........
In time, I will want it back.

Every path we cross with others,
is a relationship of its own accord.
Bless all others to their highest good
and stay your course.

Does a flower ask the Lord for mercy if she thirsts for the rain?
Not even for a single drop will she plead, for she delights in the full cycle of her birth and rebirth.

That which guides me on my journey is sacred.
Like the sacred journeys of my brother the whale
that migrates across the vast sea.
Or the sacred journey of the crane following
the calling from within.
My journey is not so different from the flowing river
that touches all life as it travels home to the mother
sea.
I am like a drum whose rhythm echoes near and
far, felt in the heart of the earth and the sky.
Felt in the heart of all creatures that journey the
sacred path of their Soul.
Yes, it is those soft whispers of the voice in the
womb of my sacred journey that calls me home.
That calls me to the Light, that calls me to the Love.
That calls me, and guides me, through Eternity.
On my sacred journey.

*The Angel of the Morning Sun greets my
Soul with a sacred dance and whispers
Of a loving journey.
As I will awaken to bathe in their delight,
I see a path of Love.*

When you dance with the sky,
You dance with all that it touches.
And when you throw your love to the wind
You share your love with all that it touches.
And when you give up your earthy desires,
Eternity will dance with you.
In all its love and glory.

Awaken the dreamer that you may hear the song of the journey to the Kingdom, and call upon the Angel of the Sun and she will greet you in the morning dawn.
Raise your thoughts to the endlessness of love, Embrace all life around you as we have returned from the journey, escorted by the angels from the heavens above.

My dreams,
They are the sails of which I ride the winds between
the worlds.
As my soul is the vessel, my mind is the passenger
that journeys and I have stood upon my ship
cheered by the angels of light.
Sailing through worlds shown only to those who
dare to face the echoes of ancient songs from souls
that have gone before them.
Yes, it is that my dreams are set as the course, my
soul sailing through the light.
And when I awake in my mind, I will hold the
treasure of my journeys in a new dawn as I awaken
to the Light.

And who will count the times I love,
I asked the Light?
Not I said the Light.
And why not I asked?
Because we only know infinity, and infinity
has no numbers, said the Light.
And my lips whispered …
Then I too shall love like the Light.

I am pure Light manifested in human form,
here to experience life to its fullest.
It is when I look at you I know this truth,
as you are the reflection of who I AM.

*What music whispers in the forest dawn to awaken
the majestic life?
These spirits of love that move like a mist in the
morning rain, descending upon the minds of those
who dance in delight of a new day.
Let us journey this day like the creatures of the
forest and the spirits of love that guide them.*

*A small group of butterflies were once having a
quaint tea party.
They watched as a bumble bee hovered over a
meadow of wild flowers.
One of the butterflies said he's a rapist!
Another one said he's a pillager!
A third butterfly said he's like an Angel who brings
fertilization to the fruitless.*

And who will see the heart of the wind when kites
fly no more.
Or watch the desert sand dance with the whirl wind
upon its body once all is paved?
Was it not the spirit of the drum that pulsated
through your veins as you listened to the music so
young and in love with life?
Come with me, and run through the forest of your
joyful memories hold your hand to the spirit that
dances to the rhythm of your love.
And we shall feel the oneness of all that is alive.

And what is an island of misfit toys?
But a Kingdom where your untold
dreams come true.

*Do you hear the music of the dawn as you awaken
to this new day?*
*Is it not your Soul that dances with you on your
path to new beginnings?*
*When we embrace the rising Sun and all beneath it,
we hear the calling of all creation.*
*And the Oneness of love touches our hearts as our
Spirits merge.*

I have known you sense the birth of the first star in the galaxy. For that is where our journey began.

I have done the work and tilled the soil of which my pain was rooted.
I have planted the seeds of emotional wellbeing and cultivated the garden of my thoughts, no more are the weeds of chattering shadows that pained me so greatly.
Now are the fruits and flowers of love I set my table with, in the light of this new dawn.

I did not know you had a soul my brother
it is so beautiful to see.
Said the ant to the elephant.
And I did not know you believed in a God, replied
the elephant, I see now we are not so different after
all.

If you could put Love in a book and sell it,
then it would not be Love.
But if what you read fills you with joy, or opens
your heart to sing and compels your thoughts to
dream, then what you have read is certainly in love
with you.

*If I were water, I would wash you in my love and
quench your thrust with the Kingdom of Love.
If I were earth, I would build a mountain beneath
you and raise you to the Heavens above the stars.
If I were your Soul I would hold you by the hand
and dance with you in between the worlds in the
Light of all love.*

I watched the morning star kiss the sunrise as they renewed their love for one another.
It was like a ritual between two souls bound through their eternity.

I walked alongside the river, and in front of me I saw a soothsayer sitting on the bank laughing hysterically.
I asked him what do you see that is so funny.
And he replied, people give me their money to tell their future and yet they know not if I tell the truth or a lie.
I too laughed hysterically at his remark, and then hurried off on my walk.
For I had seen a very angry woman with a whipping stick in her hand walking along the river bank not far behind me.

I screamed to the sky …..
If I were a bird would you love me more?
The Sun laughed as the clouds danced with the
wind.
And the sky replied,
It is because of my love for you, I'm in every breath
you take.

To listen to the song of the Sun is to hear the story of the stars.
To connect to the Wind is to hear the whispers of the sky calling you.
To feel the beating of your own heart is to feel the birth of the universe.
And to wrap your thoughts in the music of the Light within you will compel you to dance the song of your journey.
For the healing Light is within you.

Love is a vibration used to express what a flower feels when she greets the sun and the rain.

*We will write our journey upon the sky as we lay on
our backs in a meadow of love.
Then we will watch the masters of the wind create
art in a timeless dance of our story.*

Sometimes at night when I look up at the stars, I see they are the pillars of which my heaven rests upon.

As a child I could feel my Soul was connected to all things and the feeling was joyful and inquisitive.
As I grew older, external influences and opinions brought me a new pair of shoes that did not fit and said here wear these and then you can walk with us!
I rebelled, and was exiled from my social group by that which called themselves the "know-betters."
I ran to the sanctuary of my heart and spent most of my time playing in the forest of my mind feeding on the knowledge of the angels and fruits of my truth.
Yet, the "know-betters" found me, they daunted me with threats and chased me with barking mockeries as they danced through my forest with lies.
The "know-betters" surrounded me, and I was at the edge of my forest. Their chants echoing in my mind; Be like us! Be like us! Be like us!
Young I was, and a will to live I had. To survive I would have to put the shoes on, and as I did the "know-betters" proudly patted each other on the back as they nodded their heads and smiled saying the shoes fit him too!
I quickly carved a mask from a piece of driftwood and put it on my face to hide my tears. With my hands at my side as I looked to the ground in an unfamiliar shame that bled from my heart I said Yes, the shoes fit me too
And the "know-betters" carried me from my forest on their shoulders in song and glory of their act.
A thousand winds blew and the seasons changed like shuffling cards as I wore the shoes that did not fit and a mask, that hid my tears. And I grew old in a social group of lies.

*Then one day as I sat with my memories of long
ago, like a puzzle with missing pieces, I sought to
find a child with no shoes and no mask upon his
face.*

*In a distant forest of my thoughts the child
appeared, I saw him eating fruits of truth as angels
danced around him. I saw he was connected by soul
to all that was around him in the forest.*

*I pulled the mask from my face and took the shoes
off as I threw them into the abyss of nothingness
and ran to the sanctuary of a long ago forest. And I
danced with the angels and the child of my soul in
joyfulness and curiosity.*

And the "know-betters" came no more.

*If you have read this, then our forests probably
connect and our souls eat from the same fruit and
you know this page is not for the "know-betters".*

I watched the wind dance with the clouds, as the sun sang a song of love, soon the sky was filled with dancers in love.
I felt their love so deeply I was compelled to ask a tree to dance, so we joined them in a song of love that filled the air.

*Let us open our eyes to the Oneness of our Soul.
As we have slept in the Heart of God, wrapped in a
blanket of love.
Let us hold each other's hand as we walk into the
Light.
For we have awakened on a journey of a new dawn.*

Air rises, water flows, fire burns,
And the earth turns.
Raise your vibration,
Let your dance flow
And your spirit light the fire
Turn your thoughts to compassion
For all creation around the world.
The Kingdom of Love is now.

Love is in the breath of all life.
When you know this,
You will see it,
Even in the smallest of creations.

*A stream will seek the path of least resistance.
And the smoke from a fire flows with the wind as it
rises.
As the wise will listen to the soft voice of their Soul.
They too will follow a path free from the bondage
that blocks them from the Light.*

Today I walked the river's path,
it was the path to bring me home.
Silent were the trees as they watched me move
through the still air of the morning dawn.
Awakened was my heart as the river called me to
her, soft was her voice as I followed the gentle
calling of her song.
Come with me, she sang and I will bring you home.
I bowed my body next to her and cupped my hands
into the river's love.
An angel's kiss she gave me as I quenched my
heart's thirst for the long journey home.
Into the river I gazed as she danced over the rocks
and sticks that baptized themselves in her song and
wet gentle love.
So beautiful is the river's path I follow in rhythm
with my soul, as the sun angels' dance upon her.
Come into my heart the river told me and I will
wash away your fears and doubt, listen to my music
and let your body flow on the path that
brings you home.
Today I walked the river's path, her song
whispering in my ears, as my feet followed the flow
of her love.
Quite is the path, sweet are the angels voice that
map my way home as I gaze into the river's heart.
How beautiful the heart from whence we came, how
deeply we are loved by the spirits that dance with
our soul as I follow the river's path.
Lay beside me the river sings, and I will carry your
dreams as my own, let us rest as I sing to you the
song that brings you home.

The river's path I trust as I lie beside her and rest my thoughts in her heart.
And when I awaken it will be in a land of love and harmony where whispering angels guide my soul on the river's path into the Light of forever more.

We walk this day with all things near and far to us.
Our path is mapped upon our hearts and our
experiences are recorded by our soul.
Let us touch the beasts in our lives with compassion
and kindness, and calm our fears and anger.
Let us fill our void with love and the consciousness
of oneness, and let us build a Kingdom of Love to
house all things equally in our lives.

We should never feel separate from the Kingdom of Love.
Let nothing influence you that can change what your heart knows.
The journey through eternity is one of light and love.
Nothing else can or does exist past soul and heaven are one.

*What layers of darkness whisper between the
thoughts of hatred?*

*How many cups of lies must one drink to quench
their thirst to kill?*

*Do tell me the time my friend, for I have lost track
of how long it takes to destroy the dreams of peace
and harmony that once danced in the echoes of
time?*

*For I have stood upon a rock as I watched the
protestors of war choose their river of sin as they
baptized themselves in the sanctimonious spirits and
spat at others who matched a more awkward lesson
of stones and spears.*

*Oh yes my brother I am listening as you righteously
stand erect counting whores and junkies and
corporate thieves dancing in the streets to the
rhythm of beggars singing.*

*No that is not a tear I cry sir, but a spilt drink of
sadness from your mirror as I watch you step over
that toy in the street that belonged to a child who
has been missing for over a year without even a
search for him. Yet his only sin was mistakenly
being born a different color. Or the mother who
cries a child's name that has long been gone, with
hungry mouths waiting at the table and nothing to
eat.*

*And tell me again about the casualties of war as a
young man knowingly strapped a bomb to his body
sitting at the bus stop on the crowed street. For his
cup runith over.*

Because all I know, is hate does not discriminate.

*And what ghosts laugh in the street as they watch
the civil servant beneath the moon lite night turn
the body over lying in the street and place a gun in
her hand she did not have.*

*Shall we fill his cup too? As he tells himself "one
less whore junkie on the street to deal with."*

*It seems at times the layers of darkness are like
livestock at an auction being herded into a coral
and bought by the highest bidder to be slaughtered
and fed to all who turn a blind eye of self-pity.*

*I hovered above an angry crowd today, and watched
as they kicked and screamed with rage. As if they
were whipping a dead horse, an old dance of hate
reborn into their memories.*

*All because I stood before them and said "we will
die for each other's sins" and wash our hands of
the guilt, at the name of another.*

*Yet I am greeted by an Angel of Light who dresses
me in a garment of love as she tells a story of how
the garment was woven from threads of light
between the layers of hate that people wore. And she
took me to a timeless place and handed me a cup
full of love and heavenly wisdom, and as I drank
from it I saw it was the same cup as the one my
brother quenched his thirst with.*

Only the desire tasted different.

*No matter where you are on your path
my love is with you, and the words of my
soul will find you. As our hearts are linked
in this vast universe, through the great
consciousness of love.*

You cannot row a boat beneath the oceans waves any more than you can claim you have love in your heart and hold an enemy in your thoughts.

Run wild through the forest.
Throw yourself upon the back of the wind and ride.
Dive into the waves of life that are calling you.
Dance with the echoes of your Soul and the music
you hear my child.
You are the light that weaves the garment of love
for which I wear.

Once while walking in the desert
I saw a beautiful flower singing to the wind
and dancing upon the parched sand.
I asked her, to whom do you sing and dance so
beautifully?
She replied, to the rain I yearn,
I sing a song of a never ending love and dance to
the heavens the dance of my soul, and this is how I
pray for rain.
As I stood there and watched the flower,
So beautiful was the song, so personable was the
dance.
The song of a Kingdom she sang, a dance to her
God she swayed.
Like angels gently descending from above the rain
lightly fell upon us.
I looked up to see the glorious rain falling
I looked up and saw the light in the rain reaching
down to the soul that danced on the desert sand.
Like air rising I watched the flower leave the desert
sand, ascending through the rain taken by the light
she raised.
As now it is this flower that sings and dances in the
garden of Heaven.
In the light, as it rains on the desert sand.

*In the Oneness of Light we touch the hearts of all.
In the Oneness of breath our spirits merge in a
glorious dance.
In the Oneness of Love we find compassion and
kindness.
In the Oneness of Creation we find a path of peace
and harmony.*

*Our light is part of the seamless garment
of our love.
When we use our light to heal,
we are drawing from the Source of All.*

You are the song of your heart.
The words of your soul.
Dancing in the light of creation.
You are the consciousness of love and oneness,
seeing and touching all life for its highest good.

The music of my soul is equal only to the song of God.
To touch the heart of my soul is to touch the face of God.
Let us merge into this oneness in the Kingdom of our Heaven.
For the journey that we follow is in the reflection of our dance.

The Higher the Path ... the softer the whisper becomes. Chattering shadows will become a voice of the past, and we will recognize that now is all there really is.

To see the truth in a strangers eyes
is to know the light connects us all through infinity.
To see the mirror in all creation is to walk a path of
oneness.
To heal thy neighbor, is to know the Truth.

Let us ride upon an angels wings and feel the wind in our face.
Breathe deep the soft gentle love and be carried to the heavens.
Find your star and you will find the records of all your lives.
Where treasures of love and light dipped in gold await you.

The Heart is the only book God ever signed.
For it speaks all languages to all people.

The Infinite Light flows through eternity.
There is no beginning, there is no end.
Thy Soul shall not hunger, for it is the
Infinite Light within you.
Be still and allow your Soul to commune with you.
These are the true words of Light ..….

*Draw your circle, beat your drum, and sing your
spirit song.
The angel of the air will carry your message upon
the winds.
Women and men will dance in the streets, children
will say it is a prayer.
And the Poet shall record the story that healed the
world that day!*

On our journey through life,
we will meet many people, and cross many paths.
We will create many different types of relationships.
The greatest of them all, will be the one we create
with ourselves and the Source of our Creation!

*And we have been called to the table by the
consciousness of love.
To drink mint tea made from rainbows and eat star
dust bread baked in the Kingdom of Heaven.
And we will leave one chair empty to show we have
not forgotten the least of them.*

In the abyss of darkness, we will walk in the light.

You dance in the heart of your God as your angels sing to you.
Open the window of your mind and breathe in this gentle breeze of love that flows so softly to you.
Let all your thoughts be rained upon with kindness and compassion as you stand in the garden of life and your beauty will grow like the rising sun of a new day.

*If you must look for something outside of yourself
look for the light that surrounds all life.
Because it is in the light you will find truth.
As it is in the light the Poet hears the whispers of
the poem.*

*The Heart has a map that can only be followed
by those who listen.*

The Reflection will change with each new breath that is taken.
Like a pebble in the stream, will never be touched twice by the same drop of water.

Let us follow the images of shapes and colorful lights dancing before us when we close our eyes, so we can recognize the voice in the silence, and taste the stillness of our mind?
Let us open the door between our thoughts and between our next breath, that we may enter the mystery of the light and know the fullness of our journey.

*Do not fear Mother Earth stretching and yawning,
it is her body we live upon.
Do not blame the ocean or claim her washing the
land as a curse or wrong.
The wind will dance sometimes fast sometimes slow
to the song it hears.
All things are changing and we are changing with
them, this is the good news.
We come as light and borrow from the Earth, to
experience Life ………not to stay.*

*In the whispers of the meadow the flowers sing and
the butterflies dance to the tune.
As the voice in the forest calls the wild beasts' home
and the stars light their way.
It is the Poets words that open the door to the
dreamer's journey to other worlds.
For there are no laws between the worlds and only
light and color to map the way.*

The veil between Heaven and Earth is only as thick as your lack of love for all things.

*Sun rises, rooster crows and the dreamer has
returned.
With angels singing and gentle breeze blowing the
awakening is calling.
Let us wash the sleep from our eyes with joy and
laughter of a new dawn.
And dress yourself with spirits of love, kindness,
and compassion to all.
For you are the messenger of the light, dancing
with life and all whose path you cross.*

When a man dreams like a young boy seeking treasures, or sailing across the vast sea sitting in a wash tub in the yard.
When a man sees a sparrow fly and laughs or looks at a rainbow and wonders where it ends.
And if he looks to the stars in the heavens through the eyes of a young boy, this will be a man who has no room in his hands or heart for mass destruction.

If a mountain spoke, would it tell us a poem?
If water spoke, would it sing to us?
Who will see the flowers dance in the meadow?
Look to your heart my friend, who hears and sees
all heavenly things.

Dance softly in the light with a quiet mind.
Let the light be the music as you sway gentle to the
rhythm.
In the light you will flow, and sing of an endless
love you journey.
Many voices, many paths, all dancing into eternity
in the consciousness of love.

Fear not the end, for we have entered the beginning of a new dawn.
Seek the Kingdom of Love in the consciousness of your heart.

Be still and know that love surrounds you.
Be still and know that love moves through you.
Be still and breathe love, for love breathes you.

We close our eyes to the illusions that dance before us and open our mind, our heart and our soul, to the spirit we are.
In the oneness of life we are touched by great spirits that come to us.
Each embracing the unity of our reality, that we are one love.

I shall stand before the face of God and greet this
consciousness of love with open arms.
As I do not have God in my heart, but I walk in the
heart of God.
For I am not alone.
I was born of God's breath, there for I am eternal
and I follow the light into infinity.
My life is one soul in rhythm with all creation,
my love is reflected in all that is around me.
For I am not in love, but that I am love.
As I have touched the heart of this universe
and have written my story upon the stars.

We are the shining light of eternal love.
As we walk our journey hand in hand with each
other we are the breath of oneness.
Let us hold our thoughts on joy and laughter.

Each rain drop carries a song from the heavens.
Those who stand in the rain hear the song.

Spirit has no form, yet we put form to it.
Love has no words, yet we speak of it.
We don't need light to feel, yet we often want to look.
Our connections to each other is weightless,
yet so often we weigh each other down with it.

In the beauty of our awakening we rise and dance.
We feel the words of our soul wash away all doubt
of who we are.
We have awakened to the oneness of our lives and
our journey with all creation, as all creation now
dances with us.

*Many times on our journey we will meet ourselves
face to face.
We will look into the eyes of who we are through
our reflection.
Sometimes we will try to avoid this encounter.
Other times we will embrace it with love and the
great compassion.
Because we know the oneness of our life.*

In the breath of the butterfly is the voice of the universe.
In the touch of the butterfly is the source of all light.
Hold your hands out, the universe is calling and the light awaits you.

*Your spirit sings the loudest when your heart
dances.
You must be like the wild and free to ride the wind.
Be the dance, be the wind, hear the song calling
you, and you will be one with creation.*

What Spirits echo the reflections of who we are?
Do you here the soft gentle whispers of what they say?
Is that the sun and wind you feel upon your face, or is it the hot breath of that you cannot see?
In your stillness and the absence of noisy what is tugging at your heart.
That says come, come and run with me and feel the sand beneath your feet.
Let us ride the wind and quench our thirst with laughter.
Let us see if the sun can catch our joy as we race against the Sky.
Who are we to say we cannot fly, if the dreams say we can.
Who is to say the echoes of the spirit, is not the dream showing us the way.

What flower has ever sinned against the sky, or cursed against the water?
What kiss does not echo whispers of love or spill sips of honey into the heart of its receiver?
When dreamers awaken to love, it is warm thoughts of passion that dance in their heads and the song they hear never ends.

I use to demand that people accepted me for what I know to be the true word of God.
And then Love stepped in and told me
"The Truth Needs No Defense".
And I had nothing left to fight for, and only Love to give.

Raise not your fist in "remember whens" of the past my brother and sisters.
But raise your hearts to the Light of now and new beginnings.
For there is no judgment or sorrow in the Light but only Love for all.
The Light embraces all life equally and casts shadows away from that which stands before it.

There will be as many understanding of this God as there are people.
Each path leading to the Kingdom of Heaven.
This is the voice in the Light.

My brothers and sisters join me at the well of truth.
Let us quench our thirst for the beauty in life.
Is it not in our dreams we smile in touching the
laughter and love?
Is it not to the sky we look in awe at the heavens
that rain upon us?
My brothers and sisters let my words kiss your
thoughts as we dance with joy.

*Let us forgive the unforgivable,
as we cannot stand in the Light with any
reservations of thought.
The Light does not comprehend anger and
forgiveness, nor does it see loss or grief.
Light is pure love and sees only that in all life,
and if I die before I wake, I will awaken in the
Light.*

When the river cleanses your thoughts and washes your mind.
Feel the cool waters splash upon your words and baptize all that you say with love and light.
Then your love will flow into the world and awaken all the people, as the angels will embrace you again and again.

In the heart of each flower is a beautiful song of a glorious journey with the elements that surround it. For the flower knows its holy path is not in the roots of where it is planted, but is in the consciousness of its oneness with all that is.

I am not a teacher or a leader,
I'm not even a wise man.
I am a follower, following closely behind you
Picking up pieces of the reflections of your soul,
creating a mosaic of you to show the world.

*Who will love the mad man as he stands in the park
and laughs, but only the God who hears his heart?
Seek not to be the soul who wears a thousand faces
but be the soul of a thousand voices.
As only the mad man knows the soul is a prism
reflecting a thousand lights.*

Truth does not fear the darkness
Truth is felt, not seen
Truth does not fear the silence
Truth is in your heart not in your words.

Do not make oneness about you and your fellow man.
Do not make oneness about you and all creation.
Make oneness about you and eternity.
For your Light comes from infinity.

Children of the Light

Listen to the silence child,
It is profound to be.
The story before all sound,
The dance before all music.
The thoughts before the mind,
The oneness of everything.
Close your eyes, bow your head,
Silence awaits you.

Hush little one, let the wind move through you.
Feel the sun against your skin kissing you.
Feel mother earth embrace you as her child.
The air around you touches everything near and far.
Let us close our eyes and touch the silence.

*They will chase the wind up the
mountain and leap into the clouds.
They will fall upon us like the rain
quenching the thirst in the desert sand.
We will open our hearts to them as we
dance to the rhythm of their song.
These Riders of the Light that wear our
children's faces and whisper to our soul.*

One night a star asked the Creator if she had a soul.
And the Creator said "Don't you remember?
In your last life you use to sit on the stairs and talk
to me about how one day you would shine down
upon the earth in a glorious light of love.

*When I close my eyes and listen to the silence,
I can see the color of the wind.
When I open them back up, I can see the
tumbling leaves laugh, as they toss through the air.
I have watched the cliffs on the mountain's edge
patiently wait for the eagles to land.
Just as I have watched still water hold its breath.
But it was the time I saw a child, playing alone in
the yard laughing at the sky that I understood the
heart of all life.*

There once was a butterfly born unto this world
blind and deaf. Blind to all the meadow's beauty
and deaf to all sounds of the forest.
Yet she followed the light she could feel in her
heart.
And she spent her days sipping nectar from the
flowers that called to her with a fragrance that
sang upon her palate.
Twas not the shape and the colors in the meadow
she followed.
Twas not the whispers of the forest she heard.
But the map of the hand in the light she rode
upon as she glided in an open sky so trustingly.
All the shadows of the forest bowed to her dance.
All the flowers of the meadow sang her praise.
The butterfly's presence brightened their petals,
and her gentle flight was like that of the ballerina
as all life in the forest watched in awe.
Unknown to her, her wings were made of mirrors
and body was but a poem of the heavens.
Long she lived the reflection of all life, a breath
in all creation.
Upon a hand in the light she rode.
The melody of an eternal life.

When a flower sings to the sky,
the clouds dance and the sun smiles.
And the wind carries the song to
the ears of the sleeping child and
wraps their dreams in a bouquet of love.

What music whispers in the forest dawn to awaken the majestic life?
These spirits of love that move like a mist in the morning rain, descending upon the minds of those who dance in delight of a new day.
Let us journey this day like the creatures of the forest and the spirits of love that guide them.
To touch the heart of a flower you must be like the sun rays that shine upon her petals.
Let your love be the sun rays as you speak to one another and you will surely touch each other's hearts.

To see with the eyes of love
I must close my eyes to the outside world.
It is then I touch the heart of my world,
and love speaks to me.
Close your eyes my child and love will speak to you.

They say when an Angel dreams they see themselves as a poem wrapped around a child playing in the meadow.

What worlds lay between Child and Soul?
What dream maps the journey the child sings about
as they play in the meadow of their thoughts?
When is the story recorded upon the face of a star in
the heavens, as soul and body meet?
Who awakens the story that has so longed to be
experienced and felt?
Is it not that which the child sees before the dawn is
the message of the heavens?
And how many voices speak to those who do not
hear of the lives lived before the next dream speaks?

In every heart there is a song of love.
In every life there is a journey of the soul.
In every breath there is a spirit dancing.
In every child there is a poem drawing the stars
closer to their smile.

*Is it not in the still waters of her mind that the child,
in peace meditates on the consciousness of oneness?
Is it not through the creation of her thoughts
that she transcends to the great compassion for all
life?*

Mother holds child, mother loves child
Child holds self, child loves self
Spirit watches, spirit is self
Mother teaches child truth.

In the heart of each child is a giant.
In the heart of each giant is a child.
The sacred dance between the two is
one of the soul.
The soul that breathes life throughout
our universe.

The child empties her mind to be like the empty vase.
Free of all thoughts the child is not bound to limitations.
She is open to the abundant flow of love and light.
As it surrounds her very essence and fills the empty vase of her mind.

The silent child breathes deep, he embraces his spirit.
Clearing his mind, he stands with empty thoughts.
As wisdom comes to fill him with compassion for the great journey.
He will drink truth from his thoughts and find enlightenment.
For his journey will last a life time, and his thirst will never end.

Hold hands on your journey to the mountain top.
It is there the messenger waits for you.
He's inviting you to join him as he tells you a story.
The story you will carry back down with you to all
the peoples.
The story of a forgotten love that brings peace to all.

The young boy stares into the water well
As he connects to the Oneness of all life.
The well whispers to him follow the call of Spirit.
All journeys will lead you home.

Every living creature has a soul.
In each one of those souls is a unique work of
Art designed by the Consciousness of Oneness.
Each soul has a journey, a dance, a song,
And a story.
Every soul is on the path, moving to the sacred
Dance of the song they hear, writing its chapter
In the story of the journey to the
Great Compassion in life.

Who will dance in the rain and draw a rainbow in the sky?
Who will orchestra the music in the trees as the wind blows by?
Who will paint the wings of a dragonfly and sip nectar with the butterfly?
It will be the Guardian Angel that stands beside you and never says good-by.

*Yes, a seed will burst through the darkness of the
ground.
As it will breathe the Angel of the Air and be kissed
by the Angel of the Sun.
And it will stand naked and bathe in the Angel of
the rain.
Like you, it is preparing for a journey that will lead
it to the Kingdom of Light.*

Do the raindrops call the rainbow?
Does your shadow feel the wind as it blows along
the ground?
What song will play that fills a dry eye with a tear.
And whose heart will hear the silent bell toll for the
voices not yet heard.
A child hears an echo, and they smile as though it
were an old friend coming to greet them.
Be the child who looks into the pond my friend.
And look into the reflection as you listen, for it is
there the old stories are told.
Of a time when you had no questions and the
desires of the Soul were to dance.

You are the child of the Moon and the Stars, the breath in the Kingdom of Heaven.
You are the message of the Consciousness of Love, the Light that Heals.
It is your compassion and kindness that is mirrored all around you.
So let us touch the heart of our reflection and feel the Oneness of our Life.

Who will light the path of a child's dream?
Will it be the sparrow perched high upon the willow tree?
Was it the butterfly sipping nectar from the flowers in the meadow?
Could it be the frog on the lily pad in the pond?
Or is it the puddle of water in the yard after a fallen rain?
Whatever it is … we have all followed it at one time or another.

*And when you love, love as if you were a leaf
dancing in the wind, catching sun rays.
Embracing a melody played upon the sky.
Like a child who floats through the air in a dream.
On a journey with no self-doubt, but with the
knowledge that through love you rise above all else.*

I am like a child when I feel the Kingdom of my Heaven. It is then I feel the presence of my angels. For I am still newly birthed from the heart of my God.
As it is in the still waters of my mind that I listen to the song of the angels who sing of my journey.

Let us see the birth of the Angel and count the feathers on their wings as they open their eyes and lie in the breathing heart of love.
Come with me and follow the child that flies in the dream up, up, up, over the trees and through the clouds soaring with arms out.
Who is the child standing in the meadow of dancing flowers with butter cups full of chocolate and rocks that sing with smiling faces painted on them?

How playful the wind dances with the children in the meadow.
How magnificent the quiet beast is at the edge of the forest.
Whose ears will hear their song as their eyes meet in the breath of their hearts?

Sleep in peace little one.
Let your spirit ride upon my shoulders,
as you journey through your dream worlds.
I am always with you.
It is an agreement we made long before you ever
slept.

Leap into the heart of love
Blind and ignorant to hate
Dance on the song of love
Sang by soul and journey
You are the melody of compassion
You are the children of the light
Come, jump into my heart
And let us all dance together.

Let the guidance from above be within you.
It is all one calling, one dance, one love.
Wear the path of heaven upon your feet,
as you travel your journey here on earth.
In my meditations I free my mind of thoughts
that weigh me down, that burden me with
doubt and fear.
I turn my focus to my breath, to the beat of my
heart.
Or I just think about the breath of the wind in my
face and how lite that feels.

Run through the jungle ... feel the thick air.
Dance in the desert ....the sun kisses you.
Sleep my child ... the dreams are coming.
The Poet awaits you!

Rest with me, lean into my spirit, let me hold you.
Let me tell you of our relations before this
relationship.
Let me tell you why we are here right now.
Our journey is one, our connection is infinite.

Stillness is a quiet journey
Taught only to those
Who listen to the silence
As it is there, that we
Are at peace and harmony
And it is then, I am read
To hear the whispers of my heart

In the heart of all life,
we hold the sanctuary of Oneness.

Stand still, close your eyes and breathe.
The world around you is bigger than you are.
Yet the Spirit within you is greater than it all.
Connect to the consciousness of life.

Rest your head upon your mother earth.
Listen to her heart beat as you fall asleep.
Rest your body upon your mother earth.
Let her sing the healing song to help you.
Feel her love, she is your mother.

*A child never looks past the heart of their spirit.
They hear only the words of their soul and
knows only the beauty of the giants' presence.
A child cares only to share in the playfulness
of all life.*

Children will sleep with the angels of the night.
As they know them so well in the dreams.
They carry them to distant lands and far away
places with rainbows that dance and flowers
that sing.
Where the sun and the moon reach down and kiss
them, and they are loved by everyone.

A boy stands before the Gods unafraid, focused, and centered straight like an arrow.
The Elders, they patiently watch from behind, they have taught him all they can.
Boy will have to petition the Gods on the old laws of love, heart, and oneness before they will grant him his final journey.
His journey into the heart of the great compassion for all life.

In all creation there is an inner light force.
Within that light there is an intelligence of creative
energy, manifesting you to your greatest awakening.
To your highest good, and greatest potential of the
path it leads you on.
See the light in all things, acknowledge it always,
and use it to heal yourself and others, use it to help
all things grow.

*With love and compassion at the center of our
relationships we will touch each other's life.
We will lean into each other and embrace our love
for one another.
Like children and guardian angels that walk the
earth, we will stand together in the beauty of all life.*

Lay with your mother spirit my child, lay upon the earth and sleep in peace.
The Guardian Spirit watches your every breath, she feels your heart beat.
You are her cub and she will let no danger touch your soul. She is your Guardian Spirit.

Who is to say the messenger is not in a song, or in a whisper of the wind.
Who is to say the laughter of a child is not in the tickling of an Angels wing.
Who is to say the Poet's quill is not an Angels feather and his ink a liquid song.

Dance with your thoughts,
Dance with your eyes,
Dance with your words.
But most of all let the children
See you dance with your feet!
Make your walk one in harmony
With the Universe.

The reflection you see in the pond is a poem written across the water.
The sound of rain is a song that the clouds in the sky sing to you.
When you feel the rays of the sun on your face it is a star kissing you.
To feel a single breeze as you walk is but an angel's wing brushing past you.

Even a single flower has an Angel
who watches over it as it grows.

When the last page has been read
and the last prayer has been said.
As the nod of the child drops to slumber,
lying in bed.
The Poet will turn out the light,
for the dreams have been fed.

Whispers from the Heart

Today I will let my thoughts rest upon the music
Of my heart, whatever direction they go I shall
follow.
Like the tree that sways its branches to the gentle
Movement of the wind, my path will follow
The gentle calling of the Light.
At certain times, my thoughts are like an empty
glass, and I am the glass.
As there are times I stand in the sun and close my
eyes, and my shadow dances around me.
I once stood in a pasture and hugged the wind and
She blew through me as if I wasn't there.
Sometimes when I'm silent, it tickles and my body
shakes.
My dreams they come from a story book the angels
keep that they will only read to me when I'm
sleeping.
And when I get to know you, I get to know more
about me, and my empty glass fills, as my eyes open
To truth, that nothing really exists but our love.

*In between the worlds the angels speak a different
language.
It is only after we pass through the veil from
Heaven to earth that we soon forget this musical
language of pure love and joy.
Yet when we love, the echoes of the angel's words
Vibrate in our heart and across our lips with delight
In joy, in the land between the worlds.*

*In your meditation, let love fill the silence of
your mind.
Let the light cascade upon you like a waterfall
washing you free from the bondage that blocks
 your truth.
Then like a river of music that flows into a sea
Of well-being, the light will send your peace
and love to all life around you.
In the silence there is a great dance between
Oneness and Breath as they will dance to the
Rhythm of your heart.
Bow your head, close your eyes, and dance with
them my love.
For I will come and join you in our oneness of it all.
In the eye of the soul the vision is one of love.*

To journey through the Consciousness of God,
You will have to journey deep into yourself
And follow your soul.
When you meditate on the Consciousness of Love
you hold the oneness of creation in every breath
you take.
Embrace the world around you, let your spirit
dance.
Be the vibration of Love that you are.
Listen to the song of your heart that beats to the
rhythm of your soul.
Hear the Spirit of love calling you and rejoice in the
connection of your Awakening.

In your meditation climb the stairs
To the door of your consciousness of love.
Open the ears of your mind and listen to
Gods' glorious song of love.
You will enter the light of this loving
Creative energy this source of all life.
See the reflection of who you really are.
Hold your angel's hand, enter the light with them,
That you may touch the flow of your eternity.
Let us breathe in the angel of the air,
This angel that is in all life, that spreads the
Sweet smell of the mysteries of our garden.
Let us breathe this messenger of the most high
That touches every cell of our being.
As she brings the secrets of the wind
She is the angel that connects us to the
Oneness as we dance upon our mother earth.

We shall meditate on the angel of the sun
Feel the kisses and the warmth upon our bodies.
We will call on the angel of the water and wash all
Doubt in our lives away.
Breathe the angel of the air and fill your bodies
With the spirit of love and call on the angel of
Mother earth as we feel the joy in our life.

*In our meditation let us open the
Door of our consciousness
Enter the kingdom of kindness and compassion.
Dance in the heart of our God
Walk through meadows of beautiful
Butterflies and flowers.
Hear the songs of the angels as we bathe
Our thoughts in the light of glory
Carry this message to everyone we meet.
For we have awakened to our journey.
As you journey inward you find
The most beautiful creation of all.
A gentle, loving, colorful creation that
has journeyed the whole while.
Hold this creation in the highest of thoughts,
Touch this gift with your holy hand of joy
Feel the laughter and love, as you meditate
See the golden light as you greet this gift within you.
Listen to what they say there will be no
Greater words of love.*

Let us dress ourselves in a garment
Of love as we gather at the table.
We will serve each other with
Compassion, kindness, laughter,
And joy so when we journey
Out the door we will not
Hunger for the fruit of hatred.
We will clear our mind and
Call upon the angel of water
To open the gate of heaven to rain
Down upon our thoughts
And cleanse us of our impurities.
Oh messenger of the highest,
Wash our thoughts in your song of love,
Fill our now empty vase
With thoughts of compassion,
Kindness that we may dance
Together with all the angels
And we will touch each other's
Lives with gentleness.

Laugh with the heart of the rainbow in the sky
Hold hands and dance upon the clouds.
For we are the song of God, the poem of the angels.
We are the creation of an all loving energy of
infinity.
When you meditate upon the Kingdom of your
Heart, listen to the voice of your God speak to you
in soul.
Feel the breath of God touch your life as you walk
the path of peace and love for all creation.
Life is a chosen experience that continues to bring
you closer to the highest truth.
That life is the breath of love within you.

We close our eyes to the illusions that dance before us.
Open your mind, your heart, your soul,
To the spirit you are.
In the harmony of life we are touched by great spirits that come to us.
Each embracing the unity of our reality,
That we are one.
In the sanctuary of your mind touch the heart
Of silence, listens only to the presences of love.
This place of beauty heals you.
Let the warm arms of silence wrap around you,
As you ascend to the heavens of your consciousness
Touch the breath of all creation.
Look inside yourself, journey the path of your true
Beauty and you will see the truth of who you really are.
Open the windows of your mind and breathe in the
Fresh scent of love that awaits you.
Touch the heart of joy, and hold hands with your
Angels as they dance around you.
Greet each thought you have with kindness and
Compassion and embrace the all loving person you are. You are so beautiful.

Rejoice in the song of your birth,
The voice of your soul sings with such beauty.
On the cliffs of your mind dance freely to this song,
Feeling the rhythm of the universe moving through
You, as you soar with your angels and listen
To the melody of this benevolent creation.
Let us meditate upon the angel of the sun
Welcome her into the temple of our body.
Open the windows and all the doors to your temple
That She may bring in her light and warmth and
cast all darkness out.
For she is a messenger of truth and healing that
Dances with your soul and gives rise to your spirit
of joy.
This angel of the sun in all her beauty and glory
comes from the Most High.

My love vibrates in color,
because my life is full of color.
As with all of us, this vibration
extends throughout the galaxies.
When my love encompasses you
it does not divide and separate.
The vibration gently bends around
the whole experience.
This is how my oneness of love moves.

In the silence of our mind,
Let us raise our consciousness
Above all doubts.
Follow your soul as you walk
Through the heaven of your lives
Here on earth.
Let us live this day in peace and
Harmony with ourselves and all
Whose path we cross.
This is the voice of our soul who
Walks amongst the Gods.
When you can make peace with your mind,
And learn you can discipline your thoughts,
You will no longer be sleeping with the enemy.

One who sits in quiet contemplation of their
heart and their soul are in good company.
Make your thoughts a more gentle love
Close your eyes draw in your angels.
Embrace them, love them, and welcome them.
Listen to the heart of your consciousness.
See the angels as they dance before you,
Entering your heart, filling you with joy.
Go into the sanctuary of your beauty, your
deepest love and listen to the angels.
Look to the true beauty in all things around you.
Your reflection awaits you.

Do not hold your highest truth close to your heart, wear it like a garment of love woven into the fabric of your life, as you journey your path.

I am not a homeless creature; I live in warmth of the sanctuary of my heart. My soul does not teach me great ceremonies and rituals; it teaches me how to dance with my thoughts and commune with compassion for all life. This is where I live and take nourishment for my journey.

I have chased the clouds
Raced the river,
Died in the desert.
And awakened in the storm
Looking for you my love
But it is in my dreams
My love
That I see you have
Never left my side……..

Write your prayers upon the clouds and when the rain comes the people and all life will be bathed in your love for them.

If man cannot see his reflection in life,
Then he cannot hear the music in the rain,
Or even the whispers of love in the wind.

It is not the magic in my kiss that will awaken you my love.
But the beast in my heart that runs through the forest of my thoughts and pulls the light from the sun and the song from the moon then sends them through my breath into your heart.
As my lips caress your flesh for life and my love that awakens you.

A flower's concept of Love
Is not in the colors of its bloom.
Nor is it in the stem on which it stands
It's not even in the roots that bind it to the earth.
But is in the fragrance that fills the air
And the nectar that feeds all who seek the sweet
Nature of its existence.
You see, what you created from deep within you
Is the true concept of your Love.

Follow the sacred journey of your heart,
Listen to the whispers in the light.
The universe is your bridge to other worlds,
Where love is the only language spoken.

*The destiny of your Soul is not based on
your character.
Nor is it based on man's written word of religion.
The destiny of your Soul is based on the
Kingdom of Love.
The light of Soul does not brighten or darken
because of your earthly beliefs or deeds……..
As the river's water knows its journey is to join
the sea, the Soul knows its journey is through the
eternal light of Love.*

When a man can listen to the silence
and not judge what he hears.
When he can journey his path with compassion
and kindness for all that he sees.
When he can embrace all life around him
with the oneness of his soul.
He will truly be a King with heart.

Ode to Soul

My Soul is the artist, and my life is the canvas.

To sing with your heart is to use the voice of passion To write a poem with your soul is to use the voice of God. Come into my mind, my soul and listen as I whisper the ancient stories through my breath.

My heart remembers you, as my soul rejoices in our dance. Come, and I will sing to you a song that heals our world. Our journey is one of the soul as we touch each other's heart, through spirit we are inseparable.

When Soul speaks, the wind listens and shapes the clouds in the sky like a river that flows smoothly with the elements that surround you. As the quill will dance upon the parchment with spirits that delight in the hand that writes from the Soul.

Those who truly embrace the voice of soul will know there is no death but that we are life created in the heart of love. Journeying in the light of eternity, for there is no religion in Heaven. As what gets you there is not a religious belief, but a map of the soul.

Let us write our journey upon a cloud in the sky,
As we lay on our backs in a meadow of love.
And watch the masters of the wind create art
In a timeless dance of our story.

Your flesh is not your soul,
As the cocoon is not the butterfly.
But a shell, in which one waits.
See yourself as the beautiful colors
of the butterflies wings.
As they emerge from a shell into a
meadow of delightful flowers.
Then sip upon the nectar that flows
from a Kingdom of Love descending from
the blue skies.
Today as you journey through life,
You will know your soul is never separated
from love.
As you are not separate from your soul.

And what are Angels but Souls birthed in the
Kingdom of Heaven.
Yet unborn of human flesh these souls
Are absolute love and light.

Impeccable in their creation they delight
in the heart of God.
Angels are the souls that never forgot their way,
Their journey never ending, descend upon us.

In every walk of life created by an all loving
Consciousness they are the colors of untamed
energy.
As we are human beings, souls born of flesh
Created by the same consciousness.

Let us remember the way as we walk hand
in hand in the heart of God,
Born of the Kingdom of Heaven,
we are, and shall always be the souls of love.

We prepare to dream
And hold to our spirits
Of an ancient song.
We will follow a map
Of color and sound
That guides us to other worlds
And another time.
We will see our journey
Is not one of hunger or thirst,
But one of curiosity
To meet life between the worlds
Of space and time
And yet is home
To our soul.

Closure is when a damaged spot in the bridge of life's lessons is mended by soul and love for self. And the desire to embrace the journey as the consciousness of oneness is continued.

Holy is the man's path who journeys
The consciousness of love.
His soul, one with the heart
Which created all life
Gently between the worlds he will reach
To the core of his thoughts and dance
To the songs which call him to the
Kingdom of Oneness with all life.
With every breath, man is drawn closer
To the Light who speaks from his soul.

It is my soul that whispers to me
Of a journey I once took
My heart that beats to the
Rhythm of a song I once danced to.
Let me close my eyes as I listen
To the whispers and gently move to the song.
When I look into my reflection
Upon the water I will remember why I am,
The mountains will laugh
Trees will delight beneath the sky
As they too remember why I am.
Heavens and the earth are created by God,
So be it the soul in all life.
As the voice is in all things,
The voice of this great consciousness.
We are all here together yet individually.
Together through soul created
In the image of love
Individually by the song we sing
Of the journey, of our soul.

*Once while I journeyed between the worlds I found
a letter written to me.*
*Slowly I opened it, in side I found a small stone and
a white feather and so the letter read;*
*Long I have waited for you, in the awakened state of
your dreams.*
*Upon your sleep I have watched you, as the angels
chanted mantras of your birth, your heart I have
feed with a thousand lives, and your flesh I have
worn like a garment weaved from a song of love.*
*The journey has been but only a reflection of desire,
your memory but a choice.*
*The pebble you hold came from a star in the
heavens.*
*The feather is from an angel's wing whose back you
road upon as you descended through the veil into
this life.*
*Remember me when you look into the mirror of
your life for it is I you will see.*

My soul does not question its purpose,
Not even my next breath.
My soul does not question the path of a monk,
Nor the path of an atheist.

My soul only walks through the garden
Communing with beauty and love,
As it was born from the womb of eternity.
Soul is the voice of Light.

It is the voice within each one of us.
It is in the voice of Light we dance through eternity.
To commune with your Soul is to commune
With the love that we are.

When you speak from your soul,
You speak from the creator of all life.
It is the source of our birth that is enlightened
Not the human being that lights the way.

Through our words we touch the hearts of others,
As our hearts touch, our souls merge
We love our way into the Light
Through spirit we are inseparable.

*Who writes the dream for the soul that sleeps,
or calls the soul that wanders the forest on a
moonlit night?
And who sees the spirits of the desert, dance to the
music that rises from the sand.
What is the Light saying as it calls us through the
door and into eternity?
Let us touch the heart of love as we pass through
the door into the voice of light like the dreaming
souls on a moonlit night or spirits dancing in the
desert.*

Your love for another is not to be understood by others, but is to be only embraced with a delicious delight by you.

If you can touch the heart of your dreams,
You can follow the journey of your Soul,
and you will see the face of Oneness in all things.

Your soul is the highest self you are.
It is the breath of the God Consciousness
you carry inside you.
It cannot suffer or hurt, it is the Light within you.
Suffering is the physical or emotional state of the
flesh.
Be still and allow your soul to commune with you.
The heart as ears to hear the soul speak.

Soul has no gender,
Love has no prejudice,
We don't need light to feel,
The consciousness of oneness
is all around us.

The Soul is whole and complete of itself.
We need only be still and feel and listen
to know this.
Others will tell you it is not whole and complete,
that you must heal your Soul, that it is separate
from God (or Light).
That is like saying God (or Light) is sick and needs
some human form of intervention to be complete.
That is the folly of man and the rise of Religion.

It is not the poet we fall in love with.
But the Soul of the poet that harnesses the
thoughts and commands the hand to write.

What Soul does not raise its head and dance
Beneath the sky when the music of the heavens
Play upon its heart?

And who cannot feel the wind in their face as they
Fiercely run towards the sun with laughter in hand
As they jump over clouds and dive through the
rain?

Who will not walk across the waters and dip their
Cup in the river and quench their thirst with the
Angels who chant songs of love and light?

They dance upon the melody of life. Is it in the echo
Of the stars we hear the story of all life and raise
Our hands to the moon as we dance around the
fire?

To the music of our ancestors, let us touch the heart
Of our journey and see our love is now,
That our breath is now.

Hold my hands, and look into my eyes
Raise your heads and dance beneath the sky
To the music of the heavens that plays upon
Our hearts.

Who will love the fallen petal as it drops
From the beautiful flower
Or lift a piece of colored glass to see
A different colored sky?
Who will wash their shadow in the river
As they watch the water flowing
And hold a small rock in their hand
As they commune with the spirit.
Let us ask the music of our soul these questions,
For they are the keepers of Truth.

Who will hear the soldier cry for killing
The crier who fought for his beliefs.
And who will till the ground of blood and bullets
With ghostly tears of fear and rage.
What story is written upon the rocks or carved
Into the trees that tells of two brothers carried
By the angels to the kingdom of peace and love
After standing eye to eye with firing guns hating
What they saw in each other.
Yet who was looking as they lay in blood spilt baths
And bombs soaring above their motionless bodies,
As their still eyes and last breath felt a God of love
For both their journeys, tell them,
Let us come to my heart where I love you both
And we are one soul.

Man's search for this Consciousness of God
Outside himself has been his folly.
The Consciousness of God is and always
Will be the Light of the Soul.
And shall only be found by first going
Within one's self as it will then express itself
in all things around you.

What shall you call your soul
If there are no words to speak?
And what is the connection between
Soul and heart as they sit and drink
Tea while watching you dance upon the stage.
Is it not with each breath you take that
A spirit is born and a new cycle of life begins.
The desert cries not for the rain,
As he does not thirst.
Just as the wind and the rain dance
To the calling of their names.
Love knows not what it does,
But that it is and always will be.
As Souls remember not a face or a name,
It is a feeling, an eternal song touching
Hearts that call us to each other.

*Our willingness to journey into infinity is based on
a partnership between soul and love.
For our humanness to conceive this we must allow
all things to be.
This agreement is made between your self-will and
the consciousness of oneness.
It is the bridge we cross.*

To connect with the consciousness of the spirit one need only to embrace their soul and listen to the song of their heart.
The dance of a free spirit can sway like the trees in the wind, leap like a deer through the meadow.
Stand as still and quiet as a wolf on the edge of the forest and rise from the ground like a cobra.
Make the connection, listen to the song, and create your dance.

*Who will catch the laughter as it falls from
rainbows and hang them in trees like chimes,
playing music as the butterflies dance around them.
Let us hear the song of love in the forest as we
quietly watch the clouds swimming across the sky.
For it is in our dreams we lay in wait of our birth
and rest in the breathing heart of love.*

*One night I dreamt that I washed upon a shore,
weakened by the journey,
I was met by the keeper of my wisdom.
While in the dream, I stood at the edge of the water,
patiently looking at my reflection lying motionless at
my feet, anticipating the Great Awakening.*

I passed through the veil with one cup.
I was told it was the same cup you have.
When I hold it I can feel the essence of your love,
and I see the reflection of your soul in mine.
It is the cup of oneness our soul shares on the great
journey through life.

It is in my solitude that I worship my Mother Earth
And my Heavenly Father from which I come.
Angels come to minister to me the knowledge I seek.
Holy is my soul from which the source comes.
The source of all things, all creations, for all time.

Time to listen to the voice of your soul.
See the colors of your consciousness
In the silence of your mind,
You hear the angels sing of love
And wisdom in your hearts.
Touch the still waters of your mind
Bathe in the peace that it brings to you.

My brother, choose your star and write your song.
We will sing of love or cry in fear,
The universe will hear all things.
Let our paths not cross but intertwine
With all that is and we shall join the angels
As brothers healing our world.

When will the warrior's song
Not cry for blood,
But sing for love through a child's eyes.
What will calm the raging beast,
But an angel's song upon the wind.
Who will tame the giant's spirit,
But the gentle whispers of the forest.
For I tell you the most powerful magic
Is in the smallest of creation.

I love to commune with my soul,
the light within me, the voice of my incarnation.
When I connect with my Soul there is no eclipse
between the universe and I, there is only love for all
things.
Soul is breath and breath is in all life.
This is my journey, this is my home,
where my Soul and breath merge,
I feel love.

*Deep within the heart of light are the echoes of
ancient spirits.
Like whispers touching our skin, weaving delightful
joys that penetrate deep into our body.
In return are our naked thoughts that tumble so
freely through our breath and back to the light.
With angels dancing across the desert sand we will
follow them to the mirage of holy songs coming
from the light.
Just like the songs that call the river to flow into the
sea.
It is these ancient spirits that sing the mantras that
cause the rain to fall on the face of parched rocks
and dry pastures.
These mantras that ripen the fruit of our love that
falls from the tree on lovers lying in the shade as
they kiss.
Deep within the heart of light are the echoes of
ancient spirits calling to the one who listens so
gently to the beating heart of the light.
Like the wild beast who knows the spirits by name
or the flower that sleeps and awakens to the calling.
All are in union with the one who meditates on the
light, to the delightful joys of holy songs coming
from the voice of ancient spirits.*

I am neither ghost nor angel
nor am I demon or saint.
But a breath, on every corner
in every face you see.
I am not the screams at night,
not the cries you hear.
I am neither the laughter nor the joy
that whirls in the wind.
But the flow, of all their echoes
that ring in your head.
I am not the piece of paper tumbling
down the street.
But ...I am the drawing with crayons the
lost child drew, in a dream of a far away
land where they are safe.
Yes my brother, this is the dance of the
ripples upon the water.
That our existence is but a flow of thoughts
carried on the edge of the winds.
Fed by the desires of consciousness.

I am Soul
The breath of the Divine Consciousness,
The earthly heart of the Most High.
I am Soul
Pure energy manifested in the physical form,
Here now to experience life to the fullest.
I am Soul
The path of all life,
The journey of light.
I am Soul
A conscious memory that walks amongst the angels,
A love that awakens in the morning dawn.
And you my beloved,
Are the reflection of my dreams,
In the Kingdom of all that is beautiful
Of which I have awakened to.

I no longer journey the river of life,
For I have become the flowing river.
Like that which holds the sky in their hand,
whispers to my soul; come, come and be the light.
My breath was not so different then the lotus,
it came from deep within and then grew towards
the sun.
My body was not so different from the leaf on a tree,
which like me is part of the greater whole.
And then departs to ride the wind only to cycle back
into the fertilization of all life.
Yes I am no longer on the journey, but have become
the journey.
My song, no longer one of music, but the beautiful
melody of silence.
And my path, has become the sky that expands into
the universe, like thoughts that follow the map of
the stars.
I no longer journey through eternity, but have
become eternity.
A child is born in the womb of love, and it was I.
Yet, I will no longer grow in love, but have become
the love that grows in all life.

In the eyes of our soul there is no gender as there is no separation in creation.
Once we know this, what we saw as so different from ourselves, we will now see is part of our greater whole on our path into the journey of eternity.

Is it not when the rain dances on the tin roof
that we dance between the drops that fall?
And is it not when we raise our hand to the wind
We feel a pull that says "come let us fly"?
Is it not that which chooses the colors of the
rainbow that breathes life into our hearts?
We are like two breaths in one flute
Echoing around the world.

Sometimes your soul will speak,
other times your mind will speak.
But when your soul speaks,
it will echo throughout the worlds.

*Wise men will seek not to whip themselves or other
for their shortcomings.
But will encourage self-forgiveness for all.
They will embrace those who pull their anchor from
the wreckage and set their sails for new horizons
and greater truths.*

Who calls the giants to dance,
But the music of their heart.
In the field of my memories
I dance with these giants,
Because my heart hears the
Music, and I know the body
Of their love. Yes we are the
Giants dancing between
The worlds of laughter and joy.
Like the stars that light the
Heavens and light our path
We dance. Or the flower who
Follows the sun, we shall follow
The music of our hearts,
Together like giants dancing.

Young man, speak not like the thunder nor strike like lighting in the storm when addressing your brothers and sisters of the meadow.
But speak like the soft genital rain that falls upon the petals of a flower on a warm summers day.
For that is when the flowers in life awaken and adhere to the journey of creation.
As it is the soft gentle rain that feeds the flower's heart to grow. Not the thunder and the lighting.

In my sacred space, my salvation holds a meadow of my dreams.

I run so free undaunted by clamoring voices that would taint and fetter my love.

Like the eagle who builds its sanctuary high upon the cliffs edge and soars beneath the sun, they dances with the wind unafraid.

Or the leopard running through the jungle, one with his breath, his movement.

Like drums echoing through the thick air, his pace in perfect sink with all that surrounds his mind.

I too feel this freedom in my sacred space of dreams and love.

As my soul and the whale are one when he dives to the depths of the ocean and then changes course and moves back towards the top to shoot out of the water up high into the sky and laughs.

As he splashes down upon the waves.

And the camel who walks the desert and stands beneath the moon light looking at the vast space of desert sand, he knows he is one with the oasis.

And worries not where he is or where he will go as he travels through his sacred space.

For in my meadow of dreams I am all that is love and all that is love is in me.

Together we journey the sacred space of our hearts.

Who channels the voice from the consciousness of love, but it is the one who opens the window and breathes the air.
Who will see the ancient ones and hear the stories of long ago, but it is the one who stands in the light with open heart.
And who will it be that records the songs of the stars and see the many faces in the night's sky?
But it is the dreamer who awakens in between the worlds.
Yet who will believe the dreamer and follow the path, but it is those who have dreamt the impossible as real.